BENJAMIN BANNEKER

ASTRONOMER AND MATHEMATICIAN

"The colour of the skin
is in no way connected
with the strength of the mind
or intellectual powers."
— From *The Almanac of Benjamin Banneker*, 1796 —

BY MELISSA MAUPIN

Published by The Child's World®
1980 Lookout Drive, Mankato, MN 56003-1705
800-599-READ • www.childsworld.com

CONTENT CONSULTANT

Wendi Perry, Museum Director
Banneker-Douglass Museum

PHOTOS

Cover and page 4: Stock Montage/Archive Photos via Getty Images
Interior: GRANGER: 22; John Kropewnicki/Shutterstock.com: 27, 31; Library
of Congress, Prints and Photographs Division: 9, 17, 19, 24, 26, 29 (left); North
Wind Picture Archives: 5, 6, 7, 11, 13, 16, 21, 28, 29 (right); Picture History/
Newscom: 20; US National Park Service: 23; Yatra/Shutterstock.com: 10

LIBRARY OF CONGRESS CATALOGING-IN-PUBLICATION DATA

ISBN 9781503853782 (Reinforced Library Binding)
ISBN 9781503854000 (Portable Document Format)
ISBN 9781503854123 (Online Multi-user eBook)
LCCN: 2020943588

Printed in the United States of America

Cover and page 4 caption:
Benjamin Banneker in 1875.

CONTENTS

Chapter One

THE BANNEKY FAMILY

Benjamin Banneker's grandmother was a white English woman named Molly Welch or Welsh. In the 1680s, she worked on a farm in England. During milking one day, a cow kicked over a bucket of milk. Molly tried to explain to the farmer what had happened, but he did not believe her. He thought she had stolen the milk.

As punishment, Molly was sent to the British **colonies** as an **indentured servant**. After a long and difficult journey to America, she reached the colony of Maryland. When she arrived, a tobacco planter in Maryland paid the British government for the cost of Molly's voyage. Molly had to work for the planter to pay him back for her journey. She worked for seven years without pay.

Immigrants arrived in the Americas in sailing ships similar to this one.

In England, the punishment for stealing was severe. People were sent to prison for stealing even small items such as chickens or loaves of bread. Conditions in British prisons were terrible. Some thieves were executed. Many criminals became indentured servants in the British colonies.

When Molly finished her seven-year sentence, she wanted to start a farm. She found a small piece of land near the Patapsco River. She had very little money, so she rented the land until she could buy it with the profits from her tobacco crop.

Molly lived and worked alone in the wilderness. Most likely, she had no nearby neighbors to help her. Through hard work, however, she was able to grow crops and purchase her farm.

Molly realized that if she wanted her farm to be more successful, she would need help. Because she had been a servant herself, she did not believe that **slavery** was right. Even so, she could think of no other way to get the help she needed to run her farm. She bought two young men who had just arrived on a slave ship.

Seventeenth-century farmers work in a tobacco field.

Slavery was practiced in many parts of the American colonies. Slave traders kidnapped African people from their homeland. They took them away from family and friends. They sent them to North America, South America, and the Caribbean on ships. The traders sold them to white **colonists**. The enslaved Africans were then forced to work without pay. Some historians estimate that millions of Africans were kidnapped from their homeland and taken to the Americas between the 1400s and the 1800s. Slavery was legal in the United States until 1865.

Most Africans did not speak English when Europeans first brought them to the Americas. They were angry, scared, and homesick. Many enslavers preferred not to buy newly enslaved people. Since "new slaves" had to be taught English as well as various skills, newly enslaved people cost less than those who had been in North America longer.

Kidnapped African people being marched to ports where they were sold into slavery.

One of the enslaved men Molly bought was named Bannka or Bannaka. Bannka was the son of a West African chieftain. He was a proud man who once had servants himself. At first, Bannka refused to work for Molly. After a while, she and the two men learned to communicate. Molly remembered her own life as an indentured servant. She knew it was wrong to force people to work without pay. She decided to free the two enslaved men.

In the early years of the British colonies, interracial marriages were fairly common. By the end of the 1600s, however, Maryland and Virginia passed laws forbidding Black and white people to marry. Free men and women in interracial marriages—white or Black—and their children could be made indentured servants as punishment.

After Bannka was free, he and Molly grew closer. They fell in love and decided to marry. This was dangerous because it was against Maryland law for Black and white people to get married. Living in the wilderness may have helped protect Molly and Bannka from punishment.

People began calling Bannka by the name Banneky. From then on, it was the only name he ever used. Banneky and Molly lived a content life on their farm. They had four children together.

When their children were still young, however, tragedy struck the family. Banneky became ill and died. Molly never remarried. She raised the children by herself until they were old enough to help her on the farm.

Molly's eldest daughter, Mary, married a man named Robert in 1730. Robert was a freed slave. He had no last name, so he took the Banneky name as his own. For the first years of their marriage, Robert and Mary lived with Molly and helped out on her farm. Their first son, Benjamin, was born on November 9, 1731.

TO BE SOLD, on board the Ship *Bance-Island*, on tuesday the 6th of *May* next, at *Ashley-Ferry*; a choice cargo of about 250 fine healthy NEGROES, just arrived from the Windward & Rice Coast. —The utmost care has already been taken, and shall be continued, to keep them free from the least danger of being infected with the SMALL-POX, no boat having been on board, and all other communication with people from *Charles-Town* prevented.

Austin, Laurens, & Appleby.

N. B. Full one Half of the above Negroes have had the SMALL-POX in their own Country.

This advertisement announces the sale of 250 captured Africans. Today, the term "Negroes" is not an acceptable way to refer to anyone.

Chapter Two

BENJAMIN THE STUDENT

Life in the 1700s was very different from life today. In Maryland, many people lived on farms. They planted gardens to feed their families. They also raised chickens, hogs, and cattle to eat. Some people raised crops to sell. Sometimes farmers traded their crops for other goods, such as fabric to sew clothing or wood to build a cabin.

At the time, few Black families owned farms. In Maryland, most Black people were enslaved. The Bannekys were free. They wanted their farm to be successful. Everyone in the family worked hard. Benjamin split wood for the stove and fed the chickens. When he was old enough, he helped **harvest** the tobacco crop.

Hanging tobacco dries in a shed.

All members of a settler family work together to run their farm.

Life was simple, but it was not easy. There were no cars or buses. There were no supermarkets. The family had to grow or catch almost all of the food they ate. Benjamin hunted and fished and helped tend the family vegetable garden. When he needed to go into town, Benjamin walked or rode horseback. His father hauled goods in a wagon pulled by horses.

Everyone in the family lived in Molly Welch's cabin. There was no electricity. Cabins at that time had only a wood stove or a fireplace. Families used fires to cook and to stay warm. Candles and gas lanterns supplied light. Benjamin and his sisters played simple games with homemade toys.

At the end of each day, the Banneky family gathered together to eat. Grandmother Welch read to the children before bedtime. She told them stories from the Bible. It was the only book the family owned. Grandmother also taught Benjamin and his sisters to read. Benjamin learned quickly. He could read and count at a young age. He loved to solve math problems in his head.

As the family grew, the cabin became crowded. Robert and Mary wanted a farm of their own. They saved all the money they could and bought a small farm of 25 acres (10 ha). Robert and Mary had high hopes for their family farm. They saved more money, until Robert could afford another 100 acres (40 ha) nearby. The owners wanted 7,000 pounds (3,175 kg) of tobacco in exchange for the land.

In 1737, the Bannekys harvested enough tobacco to purchase the land. Robert put both his name and young Benjamin's on the **deed** of ownership. At age six, Benjamin was a landowner! The deed ensured that Benjamin would inherit the farm when his father died.

Tobacco was very important in Maryland and other nearby colonies in the 1600s and 1700s. Many people in Europe wanted to buy tobacco. This meant that farmers could make a lot of money growing it. Tobacco was so valuable, people in Maryland could sometimes use it instead of money.

The family soon built a cabin. They cleared away the woods from their new land. They planted tobacco fields. All summer long, they tended the tobacco plants. One of Benjamin's chores was to pick worms and bugs off the tobacco.

Harvesting tobacco was hard work. The family had to walk up and down the rows of tobacco plants and pick each leaf by hand. After the leaves were picked, they were hung to dry in a smokehouse.

Benjamin watched over the fires that dried the tobacco. Next, the leaves were packed into huge wooden barrels. The Bannekys had to roll the huge barrels miles into town to sell their crop.

Over time, the Bannekys became known as the Bannekers. Life for the Bannekers may have been more difficult than it was for their neighbors. Most white planters helped each other out when they harvested crops or built new buildings. However, most white planters did not want to help a family of free Black people. Also, the Bannekers did not want to buy slaves to work on their farm. They did all the work themselves.

The Society of Friends was founded in England in the 1600s. Quakers believe in living simple lives. They believe that all wars and violence are wrong. They also believe that men and women and people of all races are equal. In the 1800s, many Quakers worked to end slavery. Quakers still exist today.

A farmer rolls his tobacco harvest to town in a large barrel.

THE PUZZLE OF THE COOPER AND THE VINTNER

A cooper and a vintner sat down for a talk,
Both being so groggy that neither could walk;
Says cooper to vintner, "I'm the first of my trade,
There's no kind of vessel but what I have made,
And of any shape, sir, just what you will,
And of any size, sir, from a tun to a gill."
"Then," says the vintner, "you're the man for me.
Make me a vessel, if we can agree,
The top and the bottom diameter define,
To bear that proportion as fifteen to nine,
Thirty-five inches are just what I crave,
No more and no less in the depth will I have;
Just thirty-nine gallons this vessel must hold,
And then I will reward you with silver or gold–
Give me your promise, my honest old friend."
"I'll make it tomorrow, that you may depend!"
So, the next day, the cooper, his work to discharge,
Soon made the new vessel, but made it too large;
He took out some staves, which made it too small.
And then cursed the vessel, the vintner, and all.
He beat on his breast, "By the powers" he swore
He never would work at his trade any more.
Now, my worthy friend, find out if you can,
The vessel's dimensions, and comfort the man!

Benjamin wrote this difficult word problem. It is about a cooper (a cask maker) and a vintner (a wine maker). To solve it, the reader must use math skills.

When Benjamin was young, a small school opened in the area. The school was run by a religious group called the Society of Friends, or Quakers. Unlike most other groups at the time, the Quakers believed that all people were equal. They allowed anyone to study at their school. Benjamin and two or three other Black children went to class with the white children from the neighborhood.

Benjamin continued to work on his family's farm. He attended school in the winter when there was less farmwork to do. He enjoyed his classes. Learning new things made him want to know even more. He loved mathematics and was soon learning algebra. In addition to math and reading, Benjamin learned to play the flute and the violin.

As he grew older, Robert Banneker needed more help from Benjamin. Benjamin was a strong young man. He was willing to do all he could for his family. His parents decided they needed his help all year long.

Benjamin had to leave school, but he never quit learning. He read every book he could. His former teacher probably lent him books. Benjamin also spent a lot of time observing the world around him. He liked to figure out how things worked and spent time making and fixing farm equipment and other machines. He spent more time watching nature and reading than talking to people.

When Benjamin was in his twenties, he saw something that fascinated him. He met a man—most likely a traveling salesman—who showed Benjamin his pocket watch. Benjamin had always been interested in how things worked. He was amazed by the watch and wanted to learn more about it. The man allowed Benjamin to borrow his watch.

Few people in the Southern colonies went to school. Some never learned how to read. Even fewer women and Black people were educated. Later, laws were passed in many places that made it illegal to teach enslaved workers to read.

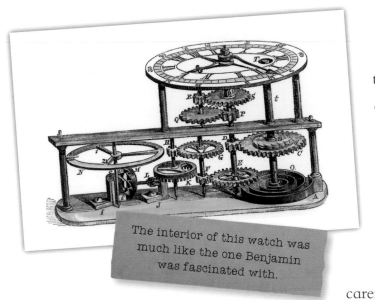

The interior of this watch was much like the one Benjamin was fascinated with.

Benjamin took the watch home and carefully took it apart. He made notes and drawings of each piece. He studied how all the parts worked together. Benjamin decided he could build a clock by carefully copying the watch.

He made drawings of the watch and then gave it back to the man. He began to make all of the parts, carving them out of wood. He made them bigger than the tiny ones in the watch. He made calculations to figure out exactly how much bigger each part should be.

Using only a few metal pieces, Benjamin built a large wooden clock. He continued to work on it for several years. He wanted it to be perfect. He made the clock so it would chime every hour. When he was finally finished in 1753, Benjamin's clock kept perfect time for the rest of his life.

There were not very many clocks in Maryland in the 1700s. In all of the American colonies, there were only a few people who knew how to make clocks or watches. Most clocks had to be brought from England and were very expensive. People came from all over the county to see Benjamin's clock. They were impressed that such a young man had made a clock all by himself. Word spread about the young inventor. Farmers in the area came to Benjamin for his help with calculations and writing letters.

Chapter Three

IN THE STARS

Benjamin Banneker's father died in 1759. His grandmother also died around this time. Banneker and his mother lived together and worked on the farm until she died about ten years later. Banneker was almost 40 years old. He never married. Instead, he found company with friends who lived nearby. He was especially close to the Ellicotts, a Quaker family. The Ellicotts ran a flour mill and general store near Banneker's farm.

Banneker had watched the Ellicotts build the mill beginning in 1771. Over the years, he often stopped by to visit the family. The mill and store became a gathering place for the community. At first, Banneker only listened to the men talking. Eventually, he overcame some of his shyness and joined in the conversations. Banneker had studied many books, and the other men were interested in what he had to say.

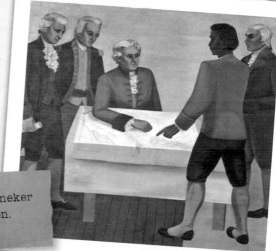

This mural shows Banneker deep in a discussion.

Banneker became good friends with George Ellicott, who was 29 years younger than he was. The two men shared an interest in mathematics and science. Ellicott enjoyed **astronomy** and **surveying** and introduced these sciences to Banneker. Ellicott let him borrow a telescope and other equipment. Ellicott also loaned Banneker several books on astronomy. With these books, Banneker taught himself how to calculate the movements of the stars and planets.

Banneker spent his nights looking at the stars and planets. He recorded their movements each night. As he observed the sky, he learned a great deal. He could tell when the sun would rise and set. He could also predict when an **eclipse** would occur. He began to work on an **almanac** but could not find a **publisher** who would print it.

In 1776, five men, led by Thomas Jefferson, wrote the Declaration of Independence. This important document ended all ties between the colonies and Great Britain. It stated that the United States was a free nation. The colonists vowed to fight until Great Britain acknowledged their independence.

Banneker enjoyed a peaceful life. He worked on his farm during the day. He studied the sky at night. Trouble was growing in the colonies, however. The colonists wanted to rule themselves, but Great Britain wanted to keep control of the land. Finally, the colonists decided to **rebel**. The Revolutionary war began in 1775.

The war ended in 1783. The United States had won its freedom. Several years later, the new country still had no **capital city**. President George Washington had a location in mind, however. It was near the Potomac River. It covered about 100 square miles (260 sq km). In 1790, President Washington and the United States Congress agreed to create a **federal territory.** It would later be called Washington, DC.

The original layout of Washington, DC from 1792.

President George Washington (on horse) works with Pierre L'Enfante to survey the new federal territory.

Architect Pierre L'Enfante left the project before it was finished. A popular legend says that L'Enfante took the city plans with him when he left, and Banneker drew the new plans from memory. However, this story is not true. Banneker returned home ten months before L'Enfante left.

The government needed experts to build the capital city. President Washington appointed the famous French **architect** Pierre L'Enfante. He also appointed George Ellicott's brother, Major Andrew Ellicott, to survey the boundaries of the new city.

Major Ellicott knew that he needed experienced helpers. He needed people who were familiar with astronomy and who could make calculations. First, he asked George to help him.

George could not leave his business, so he recommended Banneker in his place. Major Ellicott agreed and offered the job to Banneker.

By this time, Banneker was 60 years old. He knew he would have to live in a tent and work outside in bad weather if he took the job. Banneker had never traveled far from his home. He was very excited about the project, however. He decided to accept.

In February of 1791, Banneker traveled to the new capital. He used Major Ellicott's instruments. They were

This portrait of Benjamin Banneker was hand-colored from an antique woodcut.

the finest available. At night, he used a telescope to observe the stars. He then wrote up his findings and made the calculations Major Ellicott needed. In his spare time, he worked on a new almanac. He learned many new things about astronomy by reading Major Ellicott's books and working with his instruments.

Chapter Four

A PLEA FOR FREEDOM

Benjamin Banneker worked on the capital city project for several months. He returned home in April of 1791. News of his work on the project spread across the young nation. Banneker became famous for his skill and intelligence. When he returned to his Maryland farm, he was more interested in the stars than ever. With the new things he had learned from Major Ellicott, he soon finished his almanac. Banneker sent copies to a few well-known publishers, who agreed to print his work. He also sent a copy to another important man, Thomas Jefferson.

Banneker is pictured on the cover of one of his almanacs.

Thomas Jefferson helped write the Declaration of Independence.

Jefferson was now the **Secretary of State**. Years earlier, he had helped write the Declaration of Independence. In that important document, he wrote that all men are created equal. Unfortunately, Jefferson later wrote that Black men were not the equals of whites. Banneker knew this was wrong. He wrote a letter asking Jefferson to rethink his beliefs. He sent a copy of the almanac to show him what Black people could do.

Banneker asked Jefferson to help end **prejudice**. Banneker wanted Jefferson to agree that slavery was wrong. Perhaps Jefferson could make a difference. Perhaps he could make white people see that Black people were human beings just as whites were.

Many different almanacs were published in the 1700s. One of the most famous, *Poor Richard's Almanack,* was written by inventor and politician Benjamin Franklin. Franklin's almanac also featured famous sayings such as, "Early to bed and early to rise, makes a man healthy, wealthy and wise."

Philadelphia Aug. 30. 1791.

Sir

I thank you sincerely for your letter of the 19th instant and for the Almanac it contained. no body wishes more than I do to see such proofs as you exhibit, that nature has given to our black brethren, talents equal to those of the other colours of men, & that the appearance of a want of them is owing merely to the degraded condition of their existence both in Africa & America. I can add with truth that no body wishes more ardently to see a good system commenced for raising the condition both of their body & mind to what it ought to be, as fast as the imbecillity of their present existence, and other circumstances which cannot be neglected, will admit. I have taken the liberty of sending your almanac to Monsieur de Condorcet, Secretary of the Academy of sciences at Paris, and member of the Philanthropic society because I considered it as a document to which your whole colour had a right for their justification against the doubts which have been entertained of them. I am with great esteem, Sir,

Your most obed't. humble serv't.

Th. Jefferson

Mr. Benjamin Banneker
near Elliott's, lower mills. Baltimore count.

This is the letter that Thomas Jefferson wrote to Banneker.

Jefferson saw that Banneker was an intelligent and good human being. The Secretary of State wrote a short letter back to Banneker. He thanked him for sending the almanac. Jefferson agreed that free Black Americans deserved better treatment.

Jefferson was so impressed with Banneker's almanac that he sent it to a group of French scientists. Unfortunately, the scientists never wrote back to Jefferson. Historians believe the almanac was lost during the French Revolution.

In 1792, the almanac was published in several cities. It was called *Benjamin Banneker's Pennsylvania, Delaware, Maryland, and Virginia Almanack and Ephemeris*. It listed all of the **celestial bodies** that people knew about. It also told readers where they could find them in the sky. The almanac sold well. A growing number of scientists and teachers noticed Banneker. He continued to publish the almanacs every year until 1797.

In addition to providing scientific information, Banneker's almanacs had a political and social purpose. They included speeches and essays against slavery. They also reprinted short pieces of literature and poems, some by Black writers such as Phillis Wheatley.

Antislavery leaders were excited about Banneker's almanacs. The almanacs proved that Banneker was as smart as any white man. Many enslavers said that Black people were not as intelligent as white people, so it was okay to enslave them. Banneker and his almanac were one important example that proved these enslavers were wrong.

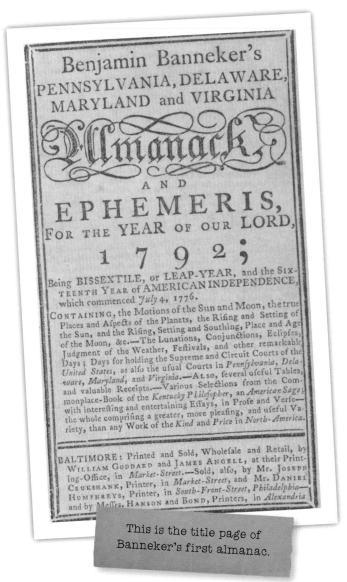

Benjamin Banneker's
PENNSYLVANIA, DELAWARE,
MARYLAND and VIRGINIA

Almanack

AND

EPHEMERIS,
FOR THE YEAR OF OUR LORD,
1792;

Being BISSEXTILE, or LEAP-YEAR, and the SIX-
TEENTH YEAR of AMERICAN INDEPENDENCE,
which commenced *July* 4, 1776.

CONTAINING, the Motions of the Sun and Moon, the true
Places and Aspects of the Planets, the Rising and Setting of
the Sun, and the Rising, Setting and Southing, Place and Age
of the Moon, &c.—The Lunations, Conjunctions, Eclipses,
Judgment of the Weather, Festivals, and other remarkable
Days; Days for holding the Supreme and Circuit Courts of the
United States, as also the usual Courts in *Pennsylvania, Delaware, Maryland,* and *Virginia.*—ALSO, several useful Tables,
and valuable Receipts.—Various Selections from the Com-
monplace-Book of the *Kentucky Philosopher,* an *American Sage;*
with interesting and entertaining Essays, in Prose and Verse—
the whole comprising a greater, more pleasing, and useful Va-
riety, than any Work of the *Kind* and *Price* in *North-America.*

BALTIMORE: Printed and Sold, Wholesale and Retail, by
WILLIAM GODDARD and JAMES ANGELL, at their Print-
ing-Office, in *Market-Street.*—Sold, also, by Mr. JOSEPH
CRUKSHANK, Printer, in *Market-Street,* and Mr. DANIEL
HUMFHREYS, Printer, in *South-Front-Street, Philadelphia*—
and by Messrs. HANSON and BOND, Printers, in *Alexandria*

This is the title page of
Banneker's first almanac.

As he grew older, Banneker sold most of his land. He was ill and could not do the farmwork anymore.

He also wanted more time to study. He hoped to write more about astronomy and the natural world around him. He wrote books about bees and one about locusts. He wrote essays against slavery and war, too.

Benjamin Banneker died in his cabin on October 9, 1806. His famous wooden clock still worked. Sadly, his cabin burned down two days later. The fire destroyed most of his belongings. His notes, the clock, and his tools were gone. The few items that were left went to Banneker's closest friend, George Ellicott.

Benjamin Banneker has long been known as the first Black man of science. Most of what he knew, Banneker taught himself. During and after his lifetime, antislavery activists used his accomplishments to prove that Black people and white people were equal.

Banneker was featured on this 1980 United States postage stamp.

Banneker helped to change the way whites thought about Black people. He never allowed the color of his skin to prevent him from achieving his goals. Benjamin Banneker was proof that Black people had the same natural intelligence as white people. He believed that all people should be free. He believed everyone could succeed—all they needed was an equal chance.

Molly Welch and Bannka got married even though it was against the law for Black and white people to marry.
What biases are at work when laws forbid interracial marriage?

Consider how unusual it was for a six-year-old Black child to be a landowner in 1737.
How might owning land or going to school impact a person's life?
What happens when a person is not allowed to do these things?

TIME LINE

1680–1700

1680s
Benjamin's grandmother, Molly Welch, arrives in Baltimore as an indentured servant.

ca. 1700
Molly Welch buys two enslaved African men and later frees them. She marries one of the men, a man named Bannka.

1730–1750

1731
Benjamin Banneker is born to Molly's daughter, Mary, on November 9.

1737
Robert Banneky and Benjamin become landowners.

1753
Benjamin finishes his wooden clock.

1770–1780

1775
The Revolutionary War begins.

1776
The United States declares its independence from Great Britain.

1783
The American Revolution ends. The United States wins its independence.

Think about the prejudiced ideas many white people had about Black people.
How did Benjamin Banneker's life prove those ideas wrong?

Benjamin Banneker is known as one of the first Black scientists.
Why do you think that is?
How would prejudice and limited opportunity affect
other Black people before him from achieving that title?

1790

1800

1990

1790
The U.S. Congress passes an act to establish the federal territory later known as Washington, DC.

1806
Benjamin Banneker dies in his cabin on October 9.

1998
The Banneker Historical Museum and Park opens near his homestead.

1791
Banneker joins Major Andrew Ellicott's surveying team in Washington, DC. Banneker writes a letter to Thomas Jefferson. He asks him to help end prejudice.

1792
Banneker publishes his first almanac.

1797
The last edition of Banneker's almanac is published.

29

GLOSSARY

almanac (ALL-muh-nak)
An almanac is a yearly publication with information, stories, history, recipes, and advice. Banneker published an almanac.

architect (AR-kuh-tekt)
An architect is a person who designs buildings and tells workers how to construct them. Pierre L'Enfante was an architect.

astronomy (uh-STRAH-nuh-mee)
Astronomy is the study of stars, planets, and other celestial bodies. Banneker liked to study astronomy.

capital city (KAP-uh-tull SIT-ee)
A capital city is the place where most of a country's government is located. Washington, DC is the capital city of the United States.

**celestial bodies
(seh-LESS-chull BAH-dees)**
Celestial bodies are the stars, planets, and other objects in the sky. The study of celestial bodies is called astronomy.

colonies (KALL-uh-neez)
Colonies are territories that are governed by another country. Great Britain governed the original 13 colonies that became the United States.

colonists (KALL-uh-nists)
Colonists are people who live in colonies. Molly Welch was an American colonist.

**Declaration of Independence
(deh-kluh-RAY-shun of
in-dee-PEN-dens)**
The Declaration of Independence announced the independence of the United States of America from Great Britain in 1776. Thomas Jefferson helped write the Declaration of Independence.

deed (DEED)
A deed is a document that says who owns a piece of land. Benjamin's name was on the deed to his family's farm.

eclipse (ee-KLIPS)
An eclipse is when one celestial body partially or completely covers another. During a solar eclipse, the moon covers the sun so people on Earth cannot see it.

ephemeris (ef-FEM-ur-iss)
An ephemeris is a scientific table that lists information. Banneker wrote an ephemeris for his almanac.

**federal territory
FED-uh-rull TAYR-uh-tor-ee)**
A federal territory is land that is set aside for a government. Washington, DC is a federal territory of the United States.

harvest (HAR-vest)
To harvest is to gather or pick crops. The Bannekys worked hard to harvest their crops each year.

**indentured servant
(in-DEN-churd SER-vent)**
An indentured servant is a person who works for someone else without being paid. Molly Welch became an indentured servant when she was accused of committing a crime.

interracial (in-tur-RAY-shuhl)
Interracial describes a relationship between two different races. Molly and Bannka had an interracial marriage.

prejudice (PREJ-uh-diss)
Prejudice is a bad feeling or opinion about something or someone without good reason. Banneker wanted to end prejudice against Black people.

publisher (PUB-lish-ur)
A publisher is a person or company that makes books, newspapers, or magazines. Banneker found a publisher to print his almanac.

rebel (reh-BELL)
When people rebel, they disobey a government or ruler. The colonists rebelled against British rule in the late 1700s.

**Secretary of State
(SEK-ruh-tayr-ee UV STAYT)**
The Secretary of State is the person who is in charge of the relations between the United States and other countries. Thomas Jefferson served as Secretary of State.

slavery (SLAY-vur-ee)
Slavery is the practice of forcing human beings to work without pay. Bannka was enslaved until Molly Welch freed him.

surveying (sur-VAY-ing)
When someone is surveying something, he or she is using mathematics to find the borders of a piece of land or to describe its landforms. George Ellicott introduced surveying to Benjamin Banneker.

BOOKS

Amber, L.A. *Bedtime Inspirational Stories: 50 Amazing Black People Who Changed the World*. North Charleston, SC: L.A. Amber, 2020.

Asim, Jabari. *A Child's Introduction to African American History: The Experiences, People, and Events That Shaped Our Country*. New York, NY: Black Dog & Leventhal, 2018.

Keller, Shana. *Ticktock Banneker's Clock*. Ann Arbor, MI: Sleeping Bear Press, 2016.

Pinkney, Andrea. *Hand in Hand: Ten Black Men Who Changed America*. New York, NY: Jump at the Sun Books, 2012.

Shaffer, Jody Jensen. *Benjamin Banneker: Self-Made Man*. Huntington Beach, CA: Teacher Created Materials, 2017.

WEBSITES

Visit our website for links about Benjamin Banneker:

childsworld.com/links

Note to Parents, Teachers, and Librarians: We routinely verify our Web links to make sure they are safe, active sites — so encourage your readers to check them out!